Funnel

Vision

Selling
Made
Easy

Steve Knapp The Sales Mindset Coach

**"This is going to not just be one of the best sales books of 2019,
but one of the best sales books ever."**

Daniel Disney – Founder and Owner of The Daily Sales supremo of over 500,000 LinkedIn followers.

Daniel Disney, Founder & Owner of The Daily Sales

This is going to not just be one of the best sales books of 2019, but one of the best sales books ever. Steve Knapp has done a truly exceptional job here of tackling the negative stereotype of a salesperson and instead shows how true professional selling should be done. I'm shocked at just how much is in this book, tips, strategies, tactics, best practices, examples, stories, it's is jammed full from start to finish. Not only is it a fantastic read, but it really does have everything you need to know as a business, sales team or salesperson to start selling more.

Niraj Kapur, expert sales coach and trainer, author Amazon bestseller, *Everybody Works In Sales:*

Funnel Vision Selling Made Easy is the kind of book I wish I had when I started in sales 25 years ago. Luckily the future generation can learn and even old pros like myself still pick up lots of value reminders and new ideas from Steve Knapp's wonderful debut. All 12 chapters are vital reading. I encourage you read Chapter 4 several items. Underline, highlight, post-it notes. This is how you become better at sales. Sales analogies are well know from AIDA and ABC Always Be Closing, which are outdated in today's modern business world. Steve Knapp introduces his own ones from SPANCOP to WOPPA. Lots of sales books take themselves too seriously and this book often has light hearted humour and visuals which adds a bonus touch. Buy this for yourself, then buy copies for your sales colleagues. It will make a massive difference.

Darryl Praill, CMO at VanillaSoft, Top 19 B2B Marketer to Follow, Sales World Top 50 Keynote Speaker

It's a classic conundrum for the aspiring entrepreneur and emerging enterprises - they have an amazing product offering but lack the skill or processes to generate a consistent repeatable sale. It can be paralyzing. That's where Steve Knapp comes in. Like a trusted uncle who has life experiences, adventures and knowledge well beyond your comprehension, he takes you in with his encouraging demeanour and tells you step-by-step exactly how to succeed. His conversational style quickly charms you yet you soon realize he is a master at his craft. Quickly you will learn how to plan like a PEAR, target SMART, implement a SPANCOP process, and make sales calls like a WOPPA. It's clear, concise, practical, and proven. Stop guessing how to sell and learn from the nicest, most pragmatic, sales expert you will ever meet.

Benjamin Dennehy, The UK's Most Hated Sales Trainer

I was honoured to be asked to review Steve's book. I don't do reviews generally because I tend to disagree with most folks. I make an exception with Steve. Whilst I don't agree with everything in this book, I do like a lot of it. Steve's commitment to selling honestly, openly and ethically is wonderful to read. I've met many trainers, and read many books, where this is not the case. Most companies and salesmen don't care why people bought from them, they just care about the fact they did. Not Steve. This book focuses on the basics and doing them well. It provides his three step approach (there are more) which encompasses the whole spectrum of selling. He offers great insight and practical tips as well as detailed plans on how to maximise your ability to find, nurture and create opportunities. This is a great read for new to selling and those who think they are tried and tested!

Funnel Vision

ision

Selling Made Easy

with Neil Anderson

ISBN: 978-1-908431-61-5

Introduction

Life could have turned out very differently for me. I could have quite easily ended up as the kind of stereo-typical cockney salesperson I've spent a career trying to distance myself from.

In fact if you ever sat down and mapped out what would have been the ideal pre-requisites for the next 'Del Boy' Trotter I was probably pretty close to having them all:

East End boy - check

Working class parents - check

Leave school with no qualifications – check

Take a Saturday job selling fruit and veg – check

Have a wheeler dealer boss that drives an ostentatious red jag and has a pair of stone lions perched incongruously outside his East End London home – check.

So where on earth did it all go wrong? Why didn't I end up as the sheep skin coat-wearing-wideboy who lived in a world that permanently seemed to skirt the doors of criminality?

What on earth was I thinking when I decided the glitzy corporate offices of Shell might be a slightly more persuasive backdrop for winning new business than a dimly lit East End pub?

How could such a start in life end up producing a man that is campaigning for the sales sector to be recognised with its ultimate record of legitimacy

– its own charter mark? It would be enough to have Arthur Daley turning in his grave!

Well turning or not, I probably think it's because – even from a very early age – I realised that a 'sale' had to provide something of value to both parties.

These days we call it a 'win: win' situation. Back then, in the days of my Saturday job, it meant ensuring the customers were buying the fruit and veg from me and not one of the rival shops down the road!

So I soon learnt the importance of (i) ensuring our customers were happy and (ii) we stood out from our rivals on the high street.

That way we got the sales and the customer got the satisfaction of fresh produce and friendly service at a good price.

But if you think about it, it's the total lack of the 'win: win' situation that is the cornerstone of every negative salesperson stereotype you can think of.

Just about every plot line for every episode of 'Only Fools & Horses', 'Minder' and any other TV programme that has hammered home the negative sales stereotype was structured around the protagonist trying to get one over on the buyer.

It was always a total 'win: lose' situation in favour of the protagonist – but most of the time he (due to his ill-thought out, underhand methods) ended up losing anyway!

If you take things a stage further, just about every sales scandal reported in the media in recent years (and wow, there has been plenty!) has had 'miss-selling' as the central crux of the issue and it has, once again, ended up as a 'win: lose' situation.

Someone has been sold something they didn't really want or been left with a product that didn't measure up to what it was supposed to be.

It's not really surprising 'sales' has had a bad reputation!

And whilst we're on the subject, have you ever tried to think of a positive role model for the sales industry? Take a moment. Write a few down. Who is that sales person you really want to model yourself on that's never off the front pages.

Don't tell me – you're staring at a blank page. It doesn't surprise me in the slightest. There's a total lack of positive role models – I just hope the name 'Steve Knapp' is written on your page by the end of this book!

Chapter 1

(NEVER EVER) SELL SNOW TO THE ESKIMOS

"Wow Steve, you could sell snow to the eskimos!" It was actually meant as a gushing compliment the first time this phrase was levelled at me. My understudy was blown away by my actions and he was eager to confirm his enthusiasm for my ability.

But it ended up manifesting itself as one of life's threshold moments – one that made me think to myself, "what kind of industry am I actually in?", "what the hell am I doing with my life?" and "do people really think I'm some underhand salesperson that would throw morals to the four winds in order to stop at nothing to get a sale?".

We've all had these threshold moments. Someone says something and it resonates like never before. It just hits you at the right (or maybe wrong) time and you suddenly find yourself re-thinking your whole life.

I was working for Calor Gas at the time and I was moving up their career path at a rapid rate of knots.

I was young, confident and – I'll be the first to admit – a bit cocky. But hey, I was doing well and no one could sell like me (or so I thought).

In fact I thought I should be sales manager at the very least (more on my over-sized ego being cut down to size later!)

I was sales person of the month – month after month after month – and, unsurprisingly, I was the person management would regularly send rookie sales people in the direction of for training.

I was totally unphased by 'cold calling' – and remember this was the late 1980s, there was no social media to research your target customers, just a phone book to find the number or you'd be on the street knocking on doors!

You really were going in 'cold'! It was not a job for the faint-hearted.

This particular day I was being 'shadowed' by a chap called Tim. I'd already got my doubts about his ability to last in 'sales'.

'Cold calling' in that era required an almost superhuman resilience and razor sharp skill to succeed.

It generally fell into two categories – a 'cold' telephone call or a 'cold' visit to someone's workplace.

Phonecalls were always the hardest – you could always build up trust quicker when you met someone in the flesh.

When you rang someone you'd literally got a few seconds to find enough of a commonality with a total stranger to gain their trust enough to keep them on

the phone. Your ultimate aim wasn't – at that point – to get a sale. It was to get a follow up meeting.

If you got the meeting you'd be expecting to close the deal.

In terms of the initial phone call it wouldn't be uncommon to:

- Have the phone put down on you
- Be sworn at
- Be told to go away (very rudely or slightly more politely)
- Or simply stumble across a lonely person that wanted to tell you their life story (and who would still refuse to buy what you're selling after you'd politely listened!).

The concept sounds totally alien in today's world obsessed with social media – a world where you can virtually nail down whether a person will be interested in your product with a quick search of Facebook and Instagram.

But 1989 was a different place – and Tim was mesmerised by my skill. He was shadowing me for a day of 'door knocking'.

There was one particular call I was on and the 'buyer' (I call him 'buyer' in the loosest possible terms, at that point he'd no intention of buying anything!) was openly hostile towards me.

In fact he was seriously aggrieved at me interrupting his day

Me: "Good afternoon, my name's Steve. Could I have 30 seconds of your time?"

Business owner: "Do I know you?"

Me: "Good afternoon, my name's Steve. Could I have 30 seconds of your time?"
Business owner: "No – I'm busy. Go away."

Me: "I see you use LPG cylinders – can I show you how I can save you some money and I'll even throw in some golf tips?"
Business owner: "How do you know I like golf"

Me: "I've just been admiring the golf trophies up there [I'd clocked the golf silverware the moment I walked through the door!] – I think it's fair to say you'll be the one offering me the golf tips to be honest!
"Calor actually hosts an annual golf day for the people we supply to – it would be really good to have someone of your skill come along."

Business owner: "I must admit I do like my golf!"

Me: "Can I book a slot in the diary and tell you more about the money I could save you with Calor and invite you to the golf day?"

Business owner: "Of course – how about tomorrow morning?"

Tim was left opened mouthed. He seriously couldn't believe what he'd just heard. He was totally in awe of the way I'd moved the conversation from near hostility to a near sale.

"Wow Steve, you could sell snow to the eskimos", he said.
"How an earth did you do it? He didn't even want to speak to you and now you've nearly sold him a gas cylinder. Are people really that gullible? I really need to be like you."
He really meant it as a compliment but it left me feeling about as low as I've ever felt. In a few seconds he'd as good as said:

• I was taking advantage of people and selling them stuff they didn't want
• I'd got no scruples and I didn't care if I was interrupting people in the middle of their busy working day
• I really didn't care if someone needed what I was selling – I'd try every trick in the book to try and sell it to them anyway.

In the cold light of day it's not unsurprising he came to the conclusion he did.

To anyone oblivious to the fact sales follow a particular process (and lets face it, that's most people unless you work in the industry!) it must have seemed I'd performed black magic on him!

But for me it was a pattern I'd followed a thousand times before.

One I'd honed over the years.

But Tim's reaction became a threshold moment for me.

I decided I needed to start making sense of my sales technique and, as a result, become more transparent with what was going on — my sector deserved respect!

And first things first, I definitely needed to ensure Tim knew I wasn't in the market for selling snow to the eskimos anytime soon (or ever!)

One of my top priorities on the visit — which Tim missed — was to 'qualify' the 'suspect'. I'd already spotted a rival's gas cylinders on the premises so I knew he used what we were selling.

I therefore knew — once I'd built a level of trust — that I'd got a good chance of being able to sell to him if I offered a better deal with a replacement.

Money always talks — or so I believed then.

I'd also have fallen at the first hurdle if I hadn't got the caller's trust by finding a commonality. In this case I immediately spotted the golf trophies — that was the point that turned the situation around and he let his guard down.

If anyone repeated the eskimo statement to me today — and I do get it from time to time from the odd student attending my events — I tell them they've got a long way to go in their studies!!!

I suggest they wipe their mind of any pre-conceived ideas of what a sales person is and start reading my book.

And if the penny doesn't drop after the first read — well I suggest they begin again until it does.

There have been seismic changes in the field of sales in recent decades — mostly due to the internet and instant access to information as well as the ability to sell online.

The sales industry is undergoing a massive renaissance and there are fewer and fewer jobs in the sector as sales activities are increasingly automated.

It's also true that 57% of a buyer's decision is made before they invite a seller to a meeting *[source Hubspot]* and a staggering 90% of every buying decision now starts online *[source Salesforce]*.

But human interaction is as important as ever in the process and – internet or no internet – it's fair to say the image of the sales sector still has a long way to go!

Take a minute to think to what the word 'salesperson' means to you.

Who do you think of?

In the UK we have two 'salesmen' that have largely dominated popular culture in recent decades – Arthur Daly from 'Minder' and Del Boy Trotter from 'Only Fools & Horses'.

Few programmes were more popular in recent decades. Both are still on constant repeat.

So what connotations of the word 'salesperson' do they provide?

Anything and everything that would make me run for the hills. In fact it's not surprising many companies have tried (mostly in vain) to give sales people alternative job titles!

Ask anyone to sum up these two characters and you'd probably get a mix of the following:

'Dodgy', 'unscrupulous', 'fly by night', 'untrustworthy', 'no morals' and 'criminal'.

So it's fair to say sales is a sector with a bit of an image problem and it's my mission to help change it!

I f you really want to upset a sales person – and I mean REALLY – there's two little words that are conversation's answer to a nuclear bomb.

Just trying throwing 'snake oil' into the mix and then run for the cover.

These two words really are the Ground Zero of insults and are regularly referred to as a "euphemism for deceptive marketing".

It you'd rather slightly elaborate and provide a cast iron guarantee that you'll be hit in the mouth try likening your sales colleague to a "snake oil salesperson" – the description for this doesn't beat about the bush: "someone that deceives people by persuading them to accept false information".

The background to the biggest insults you can ever throw in the direction of a sales person actually has its roots in Asian-American history.

Thousands of Chinese arrived in the United States in the 1800s to labour on the Transcontinental Railroad. The vast majority came from peasant families and they worked for low wages compared to their white counterparts.

The Chinese railroad workers arrived in the States armed with various medicines – one being snake oil. So far so good.

Their version comprised the oil of the Chinese water snake which is rich in Omega-3 acids that reduce inflammation . It was proven to be an effective treatment for arthritis and bursitis and it was regularly rubbed on the joints after a hard day at work.

The Chinese – so the story goes – started sharing the oil with American counterparts who were apparently bowled over by its affects.

Certain parties were also bowled over by its earning potential.

There was just one problem – a total and utter lack of Chinese water snakes in the Mid West.

But not to let the lack of a vital ingredient get in the way of a good old money making scheme – they decided on a substitute, the native rattle snake.

The American version of snake oil was born.

Sadly, for anyone hoping for a healing miracle, the potion was a shadow on the Chinese version. Rattle snakes – which were being culled by their thousand and running for this hills at this point – had only a third of the acids of Chinese water snakes and virtually no healing powers.

Then one Clarke Stanley – who earned the moniker the Rattlesnake King - ended up circumnavigating them completely and used no snake oil whatsoever!

So how did this largely legitimate Chinese medicine end up becoming such a derogatory phrase – even in the 21st century?

Much can be traced back to the latter half of the 19th century when so-called "patent medicines" – whose ads regularly adorned the back of newspapers – promised miracle cures for everything from chronic pain to kidney problems.

Then former cowboy Clark Stanley really moved things up a gear by injecting some true razzmatazz into proceedings. He claimed he'd learnt about the healing powers of the native rattlesnake from Hopi Indian medicine men and caused a huge stir at the 1893 World's Exposition in Chicago when he took a live snake and sliced it open in front of open-mouthed onlookers.

He plunged the poor creature into boiling water and when the fat rose to the top he skimmed it off and produced 'Stanley's Snake Oil'. The crowd couldn't buy it fast enough.

He quickly built a huge empire based on sales of his apparent miracle cure.

But the Pure Food and Drug Act of 1906 sought to clamp down on patent medicines and check they were doing what they said they were doing.

An investigation found 'Stanley's Snake Oil' contained absolutely no snake oil and thousands of consumers realised they'd been had.

Stanley didn't even bother disputing the claim!

Glazing over

The tactics of the UK's double glazing industry ensured sales horror stories were alive and well and front page news in the 1980s and onwards.

Even a Consumer Association survey of more recent years still revealed widespread problems with the sales tactics of many firms.

Everything from pressure selling to poor complaint handling.

The timeshare industry – another sales sector horror story – did nothing but hammer home yet more negative stereotypes about the sales industry.

All in all it's not surprising that many firms and individuals started to distance themselves from the word 'sales' altogether and give roles alternative titles like 'customer advisor' and 'relations advisor' to avoid the stigma.

Even today the country is awash with mis-selling scandals - mis-sold PPI; mis-sold mortgages and mis-sold pensions.

But before you throw this book down in disgust with thoughts that sales is nothing but the devil's work please remember – every method outlined in this chapter is exactly the opposite of what I teach.

A sales transaction has to be a win: win. Your sale has to be a solution to a customer's problem.

Everything detailed here either:

• Hasn't been a solution (because the customer was lied to about the supposed properties of the 'solution')

• Was never going to be a solution as the customer didn't have the problem in the first place as 'pressure selling' tactics were employed to persuade them to buy

• They were 'mis-sold' something.

Chapter 3

What you will achieve

I feel incredibly lucky to have lived the life I've lived. When I look back I realise Shell saw something in me. A talent they helped nurture that took me to the upper echelons of one of the biggest brands in the world.

I often think – as I stare out of my window over the beautiful Peak District - 'did that really happen to me'?

Well it really did. The cocky former East End fruit and veg seller ended up writing the sales handbook for a multi-billion pound company.

I lived a gilded lifestyle. I was promoted from an already incredible role in the UK and was parachuted into South Africa to turn around the fortunes of an ailing part of the business.

I travelled the world. I did things I could only dream about as a boy.

And guess what? My selling methods are still used by Shell – methods that can be used for any size of company, from the one person operation right up to big business.

It doesn't matter if a company is a multi-national operation or an SME; if sales and the sales force are not seen as an essential, and more importantly, an integral part of the organisation, then the business will not reach its full potential.

The next few chapters can totally transform sales in your business. It will be an area that you never need to worry about again if you follow my methods. Your sales funnel will be full – constantly. Read and learn. And if it doesn't twig first time then read again!

The truth is, if you don't develop your sales mindset to where you're comfortable with selling, then you won't keep the cash flow at the right level.

This book will provide you with the tools you need to build a sales strategy and hit your targets every time.

It roughly breaks down into three main areas:

i) **Sales in your business strategy. This is learning how to:**
- build and sustain a sales strategy
- link your sales and marketing to ensure your marketing continually feeds your sales pipeline
- build and establish effective mechanisms to analyse your results to ensure you adopt a growth mindset

Sales in your business strategy

- build and sustain a sales strategy

- link your sales and marketing to ensure your marketing continually feeds your sales pipeline

- build and establish effective mechanisms to analyse your results to ensure you adopt a growth mindset

- generate sales through customer feedback

- become an influencer in your field as a result of your success

- create your own networking strategy and learn to measure the return on investment (ROI) of your strategy – you will find the places that connect you to the right people.

Growth management. This breaks down into being able to:

- set meaningful sales targets

- forecast effectively

- identify and convert your ideal prospects

- take ownership of your self-development

- be comfortable driving the accountability of others.

Sales execution. This is all about learning how to:

- use your sales pipeline to prioritise your sales activity

- use pre-call planning techniques to deliver successful outcomes

- develop a mindset for cold calling

- capture the value in documenting post-call intelligence

- maximise revenue from customer feedback.

- generate sales through customer feedback
- become an influencer in your field as a result of your success
- create your own networking strategy and learn to measure the return on investment (ROI) of your strategy – you will find the places that connect you to the right people.

This section will give you the tools to start to provide your business with a full sales funnel. It will fundamentally change your business and the way you see sales as – done right – they will start to arrive effortlessly as you will be starting to place your brand head and shoulders above everyone else.

ii) **Growth management.** This breaks down into being able to:
- set meaningful sales targets
- forecast effectively
- identify and convert your ideal prospects
- take ownership of your self-development
- be comfortable driving the accountability of others.

Once you've grasped the above you'll be able to apply some structure to your sales and the way you develop your business. An ad hoc way of dealing with sales will become a thing of the past. You will start to set sales targets you can achieve and continually stay ahead of competition as you will become a leader in your industry.

iii) **Sales execution.** This is all about learning how to:
- use your sales pipeline to prioritise your sales activity
- use pre-call planning techniques to deliver successful outcomes
- develop a mindset for cold calling
- capture the value in documenting post-call intelligence
- maximise revenue from customer feedback.

And don't be tempted to miss anything out.

There is no magic bullet – we have to change your mindset to put sales at the absolute core of your business. You have to adhere to the teachings of the whole book.

But wow – it will be worth it!

This will allow you to dig deep into the way you interact with your customers. You will become far smarter and ensure every call and every meeting develops your relationship and enhances your sale. There will be no more wasted opportunities.

But before we continue I need some commitment off you. The teachings in this book have come from a lifetime in sales. I don't give them out lightly. When I suggest actions in this book please take them.

If you're reading this book I'm assuming you're an individual, a business owner or in a business that's struggling with sales – it can be a very stressful place to be.

So I assume you must dream about the possibility of a sales funnel that is constantly delivering exactly the right kind of business?

You must dream about how good life could be if you were getting nothing but the kind of clients and contracts you want?

Well hand on heart, your dream can be turned into a reality with the right sales mindset.

The struggle

Thinking back, it's not really surprising that so many firms struggle in the area of sales.

Let me ask you a question. How many business plans ever include a sales plan? I'll tell you, hardly any. In fact the Sandler Research Center reported that '51% or organisations have no formal strategy to help the sales team achieve 100% of the plan'.

But without sales you don't have a business – unless you're a multi-millionaire that's happy to self finance a 'vanity' business of course!

So the time has come to love selling. Embrace it! Celebrate it! Shout it from the rooftops!

And before you talk yourself out of not taking the jump think about the other side of the coin. It's pretty simple - no sales = no business. The latter is a phrase you'll hear a lot in the book!

NO SALES = NO BUSINESS

Because you've invested in my book I know you're keen to learn so get ready to dive in. And as you approach things – like so many people that still think of 'sales' as a dirty word – let me let you into a little secret to ease your mind.

If you get the right prospects in your sales funnel and know exactly when they're ready to buy it won't feel like selling at all. It will feel pleasurable – it will be a 'win win' situation.

In fact everyone will be completely happy – you've made a sale and they've found an answer to their problem. What's not to like? Is that really doing anyone a disservice? Of course it's not. Everybody's completely happy!

That's what my process is going to teach you. Sales will be a pleasure! People will thank you for offering a solution to their problem.

A problem that has been keeping them awake at night.

If you're producing goods and services people want, what's wrong with working hard to sell them?

You will be your buyer's hero!

Sales mindset success

Since I started my Sales Mindset Coach business I've already worked with over 1,500 business owners through my online Facebook Group; I've coached over 150 businesses in the UK and Europe and I've had scores of people join my online Sales Mindset Coach platform.

So many people have seen incredible success as a result.

Anyone that has ever run a business and seen sales dry up will know it's one of the most demoralising situations you can ever experience.

You spend months (or longer) developing your business concept. You plough yours (or other peoples') money into it only to see it flounder through lack of sales.

Well not anymore.

And let me tell you – unlike when I started in the late 1980s – making a sale has never been easier.

The internet has been a true game changer.

You should never have to 'cold call' in the traditional way again – the online world is the tool that can tell you where your ideal prospects are. It should be 'warm calls' all the way.

regularly go into companies to address their sales issues.

One of the main problems is normally the fact the staff are not working towards a common goal. They are not armed with a 'sales mindset' – all departments and individuals should be working towards increasing sales. If they don't there will also be discord and inter-departmental rivalry.

Let me give you an example. Lets say your sales team is doing really well, they are exceeding all their targets – business is booming. However, the accounts team are not keeping up with the increased need to invoice/credit check/credit control and therefore the money is not coming into your bank accounts fast enough. Result – your sales team are disillusioned because accounts are not being set up quick enough to start trading.

In another scenario, the sales team are again performing well but production is slow to scale up to reach demand.

Or how about, the purchasing team have not been informed of the latest sales drive and therefore have not placed the necessary supply orders that will be required to increase production...

And so it goes on and on.

To have true success every person within an organisation needs to be putting sales at the top of their agenda – regardless of whether they are part of the sales team itself. It's only by doing that, by creating a cohesion between your different teams, that you will be able to maximise your sales.

"The sales department isn't the whole company, but the whole company better be the sales department" – Philip Kotler.

360°

Stand back for a moment and take a good long look at your business.

Be objective, try to see things as if you were an outsider looking in. Consider it a full 360° review of your operations.

What's your sales turnover? Are the figures consistent month on month, or do they fluctuate? Are there any external reasons for fluctuations, for example seasonality or are the differences solely attributable to the success (or otherwise) of your sales team?

How do your various teams or departments interact? Is there rivalry (or worse) between different sectors within your business? Are the accounts team seen as 'blockers' by the sales force or the sales team seen as being 'pushy' or 'arrogant' by the rest of the company?

Look also at your own behaviours, your own values and beliefs. Do you treat departments differently? What are your own feelings about sales? Do you love sales but feel you have nothing in common with accounts (or vice versa)? Or do you hate it and believe every negative stereotype already outlined in this book?

Examining your business and yourself should help to determine not only what sort of sales culture you currently have but also what your overall company culture is. You may be surprised at some of the things you discover.

There is a school of thought that says businesses should be driven from the bottom upwards. But whilst engaging everyone within a company is absolutely vital, at the end of the day the reality is it's the leadership team that really shapes culture and ethos. In other words, you need to drive culture change from the top down.

The smaller your business, the faster you can implement change.

Chapter 4

Ten reasons you're not selling

Before we get down to business it would be helpful to give you an idea why you're not successful in selling. It's likely the problem will lay in one of the following areas and it's the consequence of not having sales at the forefront of your mind – you're yet to get your sales mindset.

And don't worry – you're not alone. These are problems faced every day by tens of thousands of SMEs.

Read through the list below. Do any of them strike a chord? They're some of the top sales fails in my experience. One or more is likely to be causing the barriers against selling. But don't worry, by the time you finish this book they won't be a problem because each one will be addressed!

1 You don't listen!

You probably hate it when you can't get a word in edgeways when you're being sold to. The person trying to sell to you just bombards you with information.

The seller might be nervous of getting a question they can't answer so they just keep talking. Either that or they just hate selling!

Either way they lose all sense of perspective of what's going on.

A good measure of if you talked too much (other than the glazed look in the eyes of the potential buyer!) is that you've spoken for 70%+ of the meeting.

Your goal is a maximum of 30% talking.

2 You don't prepare

Have you ever left a sales meeting and, when you're on the way back to the office, you say to yourself "that's what I meant to ask" and consoled yourself with "oh I'll cover it next time"?

The reality is you haven't planned. I was recently at an evening networking event and 15 business owners who were going to do sales calls the next morning admitted, by a show of hands, that they had not prepared properly.

I mean come on, do you really deserve to succeed? Do you really not value your time, your clients' time, the opportunity that sales might bring? Of course you do, so why do you act so unprofessionally?

Using a simple pre call plan – which we'll be covering later in the book - can ensure you don't waste time, you get better sales outcomes and you look professional.

3 You don't record what happened before

A powerful start to a follow up meeting is "just to recap on what we agreed previously".

Do you hear yourself starting off with that?

No? Do you end up meandering chaotically over previously trodden ground trying desperately to remember what happened before? Are you surprised you aren't closing deals – really!?

Folks - write things down and confirm them during and at the end of a meeting; then follow up with an email if appropriate.

Being clear on any next steps, who's doing what and where you are in the sales process is basic stuff. But you're too busy, right? Or you've just got a good memory... who are you kidding? Not me! We'll be going into the 'post call report' later in the book. We need these steps to be a natural part of your day.

4 You ask for the order too early

Now here's a thing that regularly happens because you don't follow a sales process.

Put yourself in a buyer's shoes.

Have you ever had those wonderful experiences when you're being sold to but it doesn't feel like you're being sold to?

That's because the seller is moving through a sales process that matches to your buying process... it's not difficult. When it feels bad it's because you are running separate races and you're not in tune with where you both are in the sales process.

If you don't follow a sales process, how do you really know where the sale is up to? I mean, you could be negotiating when your prospect is still analysing options...

Or you could be closing before a buyer is ready.

Don't try to argue that you don't need a process. If you don't have a sales process you can't learn why you win, where you lose or where your offer is strong or weak.

In this book you will learn the seven steps of the buying process. Every journey follows the same pattern. There really is no mystery to it!

5 Your offer is way past its sell by date

Sorry to tell you this but actually what you're selling just isn't good enough anymore. It might have been once but not any longer. Don't say it can't happen to you – it can and it will so be prepared!

You haven't updated it, refreshed it. You're out of kilter with prices and your solutions are so yesterday. Don't wait until your offer becomes fashionable again, you'll be out of business!

It's time to dust down what you're selling and make it relevant and fresh. It's time to stand back and work out what your customer is buying.

6 You don't differentiate

I know, I know, you don't have to market your business, you're not on social media and everybody knows what you do. I've heard it all before.

I love businesses like you... Well I love to win business from businesses like you.

You have to differentiate. You have to stand out. You have to shout about what you do.

How can your prospective customers see you through the fog of sameness if you're not shining like a beacon?

Don't hide your light under a bushell. Work out where you win, work out why you win and differentiate in your offers and marketing.

Selling will become easier because your prospects are excited to be buying from someone who is better than everybody else out there. It's a simple fact of life.

7 Are you tired and boring?

I mean look at you! When was the last time that website, brochure, presentation was refreshed?

Imagine at the bottom of that brochure you've still got your fax number, Google+ ... what is this saying?

Also, are you still excited about what you sell, the problems you solve? If you're not why the heck should your potential buyer be? The only way you'll energise your potential customers is by being energized by your own business yourself.

Come on, you can tell me. Are you on your A game? If the answer is no then you have to wake up – now!

8 You don't offer value and you jump to price

It's never been easier to sell...

Yep I just said that! I believe with the access to information and the internet it has never been easier to sell.

But let me qualify that. I don't believe it's easier to sell value. That's harder because you have to know your sector or segment and product.

You have to know your industry, the players, the changing trends.

You need to understand how your offer adds a value over and above your competition so you can charge what you want to charge. You're worth it right?

What's easier to do is commoditise your products, your brand, yourself... jumping straight to price is a road to ruin. If you discount your price by 10% you have to sell a lot more than 10% to just stand still. Discounting can be nothing but a race to the bottom.

Selling should be fun when you're adding value and being paid for the value you add. Make people proud to buy into your brand and pay your prices!

9 You don't differentiate sales and marketing

Sometimes you actually forget to sell and that's one of the reason things don't happen. Yep, what you actually do is you get suckered in to the marketing side and think everything is about being visible and creating tribes and cramming lists and creating automation.

Sorry folks, but this is the wrong train. Do all those things for sure but make sure you sell.

What do I mean? Your call to action must be explicit, a direction to a product, a sign to a next step, an offer to take the conversation to the next stage.

From here you feed your sales funnel and sell!

10 You don't network where your ideal clients hang out

Networking can be fun and I actually think being able to network with people you like is a true pleasure of being in business. But you need to ensure you're networking at events where your target clients are hanging out.

It's too easy at the end of the month to see you've spent £150 on networking and all you've done is put mileage on the car, got rid of some business cards and put on a bit of weight from the breakfasts and lunches on offer.

Step back and have a strategy that connects you to the right people or at least one that gets you seen in the eco system of the people that need to know.

Also, don't turn down the opportunities to speak and stand out from the crowd. Networking is part of your marketing mix and it helps you position yourself as the go to person.

Last point for networking... follow up, yes if somebody has shown interest and you've exchanged cards, then follow up. It's alarming how many of you just don't follow up.

Chapter 5

Building a bullet-proof sales strategy

et's get one thing straight before we start. Being good at sales isn't tantamount to have mastered the dark arts. When you look back at the end of this book you'll realise effective sales is nothing more than straight forward, common sense.

Follow my teachings and you'll wonder just how and why sales ever managed to attract such a negative stereotype! It's not as if anyone can really avoid it! People have been selling since the dawn of time.

No sales = no business - it's really that simple! You don't really have any choice in the matter if you're running your own business – so you might as well get comfortable with it and stop it being something that brings about negative connotations!

In this section we are really going to start to get down to business as we consider how we:
- build and sustain a sales strategy
- link your sales and marketing to ensure your marketing activity continually feeds your sales pipeline
- build and establish effective mechanisms to analyse your results, adopting a growth mindset
- generate sales through customer feedback
- become an influencer in your field as a result of your success
- create your own networking strategy and learn to measure the return on investment (ROI) of your actions – you will find the places that truly connect you to the right people.

The Sales Plan

The first thing you need to design is your 'sales plan'.

Put simply, it's the 'big picture'. It's what you want your business to look like and what you want it to achieve.

It's your direction of travel and it keeps everything on track.

Without a sales plan, well, you are leaving everything to pure luck and you're likely to come unstuck very quickly or loose your business altogether! It's a recipe for stress and chaos.

I draw an easy analogy with gardening.

Imagine you have a garden that is just soil and you want to transform it with beautiful flowers and trees.

You want it to be something you're proud of and can admire.

So what would you do to achieve this? Well you wouldn't just start planting – would you? Of course you wouldn't. Not unless you want it to look arguably worse than the barren piece of soil you started with.

You would first of all think about what kinds of flowers and trees you wanted, and where you wanted them. You'd plant at the optimum time for each seed, you'd map everything out, you'd be meticulous.

And even when everything had grown you would tend it regularly, weeding, trimming and watering.

It's a similar process with your sales plan.

Make things easy with P.E.A.R. planning

Does the thought of making a plan fill you with dread? Well it shouldn't. Having a plan gives you a road map. It should always make the process easier – especially if you follow a tried and tested system.

P.E.A.R. planning is a process that will avoid your plan going pear-shaped! It breaks down as follows:

P is for the Plan:

• Your route to market:

Your route to market is defined by your objectives. These can be found by asking yourself the following questions:

• What do you want – and why?
• When do you want it? 12 months? 2 years? 10 years?
• What will you do when things don't go to plan?
• How big do you want to grow?

What do you want – and why?	
When do you want it? 12 months? 2 years? 10 years?	
What will you do when things don't go to plan?	
How big do you want to grow?	
How quickly do you want to grow?	
Are you aiming to be mainstream?	
If you're in a niche market – which one does your product sit in?	
Are you setting out to sell direct or online – or both?	

- How quickly do you want to grow?
- Are you aiming to be mainstream?
- If you're in a niche market – which one does your product sit in?
- Are you setting out to sell direct or online – or both?

If you haven't already asked these questions then don't delay. The answers shape everything going forward.

You may find other questions coming to the surface that are pertinent to your business and/or personal life goals. Jot everything down.

• Sales targets

Just like defining your objectives - you must also have targets to aim for. They can be for both your personal life and your business. They are normally closely related.

Don't be tempted to simply pluck a number or date out of the air. These targets need to be right – and they need to be achievable!

We will be diving into this in detail later in the book – for now we're going to consider useful target areas we'll be using.

These are:

Money: How much money do you want to make? This is usually not the main target but it will help you reach any personal goals that you may have – like paying off your mortgage or buying a new car.

Units sold: This target is easier to define. How many units do you have to sell to make the money you want? Are you selling your time? If so, how much time do you have to sell?

Time: How much time are you giving to reach your targets? How long will it take? 3, 6, 12 months, 2 years maybe? These figures will obviously depend on your product, the volumes involved and if you're selling your time.

Costs: Although this is not strictly a target, it does feed into your target setting and is very important. You need to know how much your product costs to make to be able to work out how much profit you want to make for each product. This then determines how many units you have to sell to reach your financial target.

Goals: Goals are not strictly targets in themselves – they are generally more aspirational. They are normally the reason you went into business in the first place, or maybe they're a long held dream. You ignore these at your peril – these are normally the things that drive your targets.

iii) Sales Tactics – how do your products stack up?

Sales tactics are probably not what you might be thinking. They're not about how you 'undercut the competition' or getting one over on your main rival!

They relate to your product and how you will be selling it.

Your particular business could break down into:

• **Low Volume / High Cost** – this simply means the items you're selling have high profit margins and you don't have to sell that many of them to hit your profit targets

• **High Volume / Low Cost** – this means the products you sell have low profit margins and you have to sell vast quantities to hit your profit targets.

Once you have defined where your product sits in the volume/cost ratio, you have an important piece of the puzzle in place. This will feed back into your target setting as it is an integral part of that activity.

Where does your product sit? Have you considered this before? You need to.

• Budgets

It's essential to know how much you are willing and able to invest in your sales and marketing. Your budget must not only be reasonable but must be sustainable over the short, medium and long term.

This is one very important area where you can't avoid doing the maths. Failure to look at budgets can lead to spending which has no direction, or even no spending when it is definitely needed.

It's really easy to lose sight of how much you are spending in your business if you don't set a budget up front.

For example – you have set a target to make £15K turnover in sales over the next six months which will give you a healthy £5K profit. You achieve it and then look back to see how healthy your balance sheet is – and find that you spent £5k on creating a website, Facebook ads and promotional literature – wiping out the profit.

Maybe you recognise this from your own experience?

There are a couple of things to consider when looking at planning your budgets These are:

– Will your sales recoup the budget spend?

– Will your sales provide for future budget spend?

All in all, this adds up to good old common sense. Weighing up the spending against the gains. Time to check if you have any budgets set in your business!

• Marketing

Marketing is all about how you make your products and services visible to your customers. It has to be linked to your sales outcomes and targets. And you always need to keep an eye on budgets.

Where will you do your marketing? Online, social media, advertising – there are so many different ways on offer. You need to find the ones that are right for you.

And there's another thing to think about – where does your target audience

or audiences hang out? For example, if your product is a business to customer item (B2C), then networking at events that have lots of business owners is not a good use of your marketing time. Whereas, a well placed advert for your product in a suitable magazine or on Facebook may be totally appropriate.

Marketing and sales are two sides of the same coin — and each must reflect the other, like having two hands on a steering wheel, working together to reach their destination.

We will cover the relationship between marketing and sales later in this book.

So take a moment to think right now, do you have a marketing plan? is your marketing plan hitting the mark?

E is for Execute:

Now you have your plan it's time to put it into action and execute — nothing happens without action. And there are lots of things you can do to make sure that action is taken.

Ensure everything is planned in your calendar — dates, times, who, what and where.

And set reminders — that way you will be able to ensure everything runs smoothly and you will not become overwhelmed.

Dates and times: Run your plan like an efficient machine – it may feel strange at first but before you know it – it will be second nature to make those calls, record those sales and update that CRM spreadsheet!

Line up those ducks: Make sure that anyone that is part of your plan knows what they need to do and when! Even when you are a one person business you will be collaborating and relying on others to get things done. Take the lead and be very clear on what everyone's tasks and responsibilities are. Follow up and check that stuff has been done.

A is for Adapt:

No matter how comprehensive your plan, you need to be able to change and adapt when things change. And you also need to keep an eye on the trends to adapt quickly and make sure your product does not get left behind.
There are two main things to consider that will help you adapt and flex to trends and changes.

Being the expert:

Are you a member of a trade association, or meet regularly with others who do what you do?
 Do you subscribe to relevant publications or get regular refresher training?
 Whatever your business, there will be opportunities for you to stay close to what is happening and learn from others. It is absolutely essential you keep up to date with changes and trends in your sector.

Feedback:

It is absolutely imperative you capture and use customer feedback.
This rich source of information will help you follow what customers are demanding and where you can make changes to your products to improve them. It might even give you the knowledge and confidence to innovate and broaden your product range to cover more customer sectors.
 Some big businesses have gone under because they didn't keep up with the world that was changing around them – look at Blockbuster.
 And others have moved with the times and continue to succeed – just look at Apple and Emirates Airlines who have been innovative in their products, keeping ahead of the customer demand.

R is for Review:

Nothing stays the same for long so review, review, review!

Even the best laid plans can soon go out of date. So making a point of reviewing your sales plan is a must to keep it fresh and relevant.

Forecasting is another essential part of your review cycle. You have already set your targets so you know what you want to achieve. If it's 10,000 widgets by the end of quarter one then you will need to review that at the beginning of quarter two.

It's not just about reviewing targets – you should review all of your plans on a regular basis.

How often do you review?

Monthly? Quarterly, Yearly? Well it depends on your sales tactics strategy.

If your strategy is high volume/low cost then reviewing often is useful – you can then make changes quickly to ensure you keep the high volume going.

If it's low volume/high cost then your review cycle could be less often as you will only be able to determine trends over the longer term.

Whatever you decide is best for your business – make it happen.

Chapter 6

Networking – a necessary evil

Networking is, without a doubt, one of the most effective ways to grow your business. There's no avoiding it if you want to build a truly effective sales funnel.

I know that from (bitter) personal experience. Within my role at Shell I had leveraged the most amazing worldwide network possible.

I'd literally thousands of people at my fingertips at all levels: from the upper echelons of leadership down to the foot soldiers. I felt valued, protected and my expertise was constantly in demand.

If I needed help it was but an email or phonecall away.

It never occurred to me just how different life would be on the outside as I launched my own business.

I had no external network whatsoever. I therefore had no sales funnel, no one to protect me and value me in the business world. I was totally alone.

Life outside the cossetted world of Shell was a big shock.

It took a full two years to create a similar network to support my own business. And it was all done through networking – both face-to-face and online.

Like it or loathe it – it is an absolutely essential part of business. You are unlikely to succeed without it. Did you know that 85%* of jobs are filled through networking? And, added to that, 72%* of people also say one of strongest and most positive impressions they can have of someone is made by their appearance and handshake. We're only human after all! *Source – virgin.com*

So many people get networking all wrong and that's why they don't get the results.

Face-to-face is undoubtedly the best way to build instant trust but you'll only get results if you follow these simple rules at your networking events:

• **Show up early!** At a networking event it's a much better strategy to arrive early as being one of the first attendees allows you to have the choice of who to talk to as people won't have settled into groups.

• **Ask easy questions.** To get the conversation started, simply walk up to a person or a group, and say, "May I join you" or "What brings you to this event?" Don't forget to listen intently to their replies. If you're not a natural extrovert, you're probably a very good listener and listening can be an excellent way to get to know a person.

• **Ditch the sales pitch.** Remember, networking is all about relationship building. You don't need to do the hard sell within minutes of meeting a person. If a potential customer does ask you about your product or service, be ready with

an easy description of your company and be able to explain the value you've delivered to other companies.

• **Share your passion**. Win people over with your enthusiasm for your product or service. Leave a lasting impression by telling a story about why you were inspired to create your company. Talking about what you enjoy is regularly contagious.

• **Smile.** It's a simple rule of engagement. By smiling, you'll put your nervous self at ease, and you'll also come across as warm and inviting to others. Remember to smile before you enter the room, or before you start your next conversation.

• **Don't hijack the conversation.** Think about the most successful networkers you've met. It's likely they're good at making other people feel special. That's why they're successful. Copy their traits. Look people in the eye, repeat their name, listen to what they have to say, and suggest topics that are easy to discuss. Be a conversationalist, not a talker.

• **Remember to follow up.** It's often said that networking is where the conversation begins, not ends. If you've had a great exchange, ask your conversation partner the best way to stay in touch. Some people like email or phone; others prefer social networks like LinkedIn. Get in touch within 48 hours of the event.

But before you dive into any of the above, there's something you need to do to help you find your ideal networking groups...

You need to find your target customer.

Complete the following table. Do it to the best of your ability. You may have different customer profiles for different goods and services so you may need to do more than one.

Male or female	Age range
What's their background story?	
What problems do they have that your goods or services can solve?	
Are they in a position to buy and what is their budget?	
Where do they hang out?	
Where can I reach them?	

The best places to network

Networking can take place both online or in the real world. Ideally you should be doing both. Work through the following table to give you more insight into your business and where the best places to network are likely to be.

Location	Yes/ No	Where
B2B		
B2C		
LinkedIn		
Facebook		
Twitter		
Industry specific groups		

The business world is awash with networking events. Just give Google or LinkedIn a quick search. But it's all about finding the ones that have your target clients amongst the audience and ensuring you're prepared so you always make the best impression.

Don't be afraid to try a few out. You might even want to start your own! I've had lots of colleagues that have done this very successfully. They provide amazing sales funnels!

Chapter 7

Implementing your strategy for growth

So congratulations are in order – your sales strategy is now written. You now have a major building block in place. This will be the cornerstone of everything moving forward.

You would not believe just how many businesses don't have this.

But before you crack open the champagne there's a bit more to go – in fact quite a lot.

So lets settle for a cup of tea, a pat on the back and then sit yourself back down and we'll crack on.

Hey – you don't want to be mediocre now do you? Of course you don't – you're going to nail this sales thing! All of it!

So the next piece of the jigsaw is answering the question:

"Where do I find the sales and how do I keep them increasing?"

How to identify and convert your ideal prospects

'Prospect' is a word you'll hear me say a lot in this book. They are the lifeblood of sales. They are the people you know that could be turned into a paying customer.

Ever spent hours chasing a new piece of business only to be told the person you've been dealing with doesn't have the authority to spend the money?

That's because the person wasn't a true 'prospect' – we need to ensure that never happens again!

So let's first of all define what we mean by 'prospect'. For most people the word conjures up visions of a miner panning for gold in the American West.

Their entire life was focused on one thing – finding gold.

Well, my definition is not a million miles away – stands to reason right? A prospect is a potential customer who wants to buy – they have the gold you are looking for.

You just need to find them!

So how do you know where to look for your prospects?

And even more importantly – who are your Ideal prospects?
Well not all prospects are created equal so how do you know who is who?

Building your prospect profiles

Effective sales is all about effective planning. So if you've done your research and understand what your ideal prospect looks like, then it stands to reason you'll know exactly how to act when someone comes along that fits that profile. You'll be ready to listen as you're already confident you can solve their problem.

You'll also be able to:

Anticipate their needs

Deliver specific, relevant, targeted services

Shorten the order to delivery time as you will be prepared in advance.

This is by far the most efficient way to spend your time when connecting to people at networking events or deciding on how to spend your marketing budget.

You will target your efforts to attract your ideal prospect.

Building profiles of these people is like building your very own game of 'Who's Who?' and it pays massive dividends.

So lets go ahead and create your first one.

Here are the questions you need to ask yourself to help you:

• **Is your prospect male or female – does your product or service appeal to both sexes?**
Your prospects will be both men and women so make sure you consider sexes first. Depending on your business this may be very important. For example, if you sell pamper products then the different sexes may have different problems and reasons to buy. You have to consider both carefully.

• **How old is your ideal prospect?**
The profiles should cover a number of age ranges. Reasons to buy and how your product solves their problem may be different if they are 30 or 50 years old.

• **What problem does your prospect have?**
Your product will solve a number of problems so make sure that each profile has one of these problems attached to it - just choose the one that is most apt for that profile. For example, if you provide personal fitness training then make a list of all of the reasons people come to you for help and create a typical profile for each of them. A person in their 20s will have different needs to someone in their 60s.

• **Is your prospect in a position to buy?**
When you create your profiles you will need to consider if someone has the power to buy. This is especially important if you are a B2B business. What position in the company will a person need to have to give them the authority?

• **Where do your prospects hang out?**
Which social media platforms do they use? Are they members of a networking group? Do your research and find where you can reach them.

Prospect examples

So here's what a couple of prospect profiles could look like – but remember, the amount of research you need to do to build up your prospect profiles will depend on the business you are in.
You may need to dig down much, much deeper.

You need to set aside a good chunk of time for this profile building exercise – enrol the help of others if you want to. If you're already in business dig down into the types of people that have bought from you previously. If you're a new business have a look at the kinds of people that are clients of businesses that you'd consider competitors or in similar industries.

A) Prospect profile for Ms A.

Male or female: Female   **Age range:** Ms A is between 30 and 45

Background story:
Ms A is a career woman with a long term partner and no children

The problem:
Ms A is responsible for the regulatory required training where she works. Ms A struggles to get the training completed by everyone in the company on time.

Ability to buy:
Ms A has a budget and can authorise up to £2K per year. She can apply for more.

Where do they hang out:
Ms A is active on Linkedin and is a member of a couple of HR groups

B) Prospect profile for Mr B.

Male or female: Male   **Age range:** Mr B is 45 to 55 years old

Background story:
Mr B has been running his building company for 15 years. A workaholic, he only has time for his business.

The problem:
Mr B wants to expand his business but struggles to understand the apprenticeship schemes and how to implement them.

Ability to buy:
He has a budget and could benefit from knowing about the apprenticeship levy.

Where do they hang out:
Mr B likes traditional face to face contact and is a member of the local Chamber of Commerce as well as the Association of Master Builders.

Who are your best customers?

If you're already in business you may have your ideal customer profile (or profiles) staring you in the face.

Knowing who your best customers are is one way of identifying your ideal prospects. Think of the way Facebook creates a duplicate audience – it's applying the same principle.

If you already have customers who come back time and again then it's useful to work out why and who they are.

What characteristics do these customers share that you can look for when assessing possible prospects?

Here are some questions you could ask yourself – and your customers – to create that picture.

● **Who are they in their business?'**
If you are B2B selling then who in that business is buying from you?
When you know this you can target that same role in similar businesses as a prospect.

● **What problem does your product solve for them?**
It's useful to know exactly the problem that has been solved by your product. You can then target people and businesses with the same problem.

● **How did they hear about you in the first place?**
There may be a trend that emerges from asking this question which will help you target your marketing. It will certainly point you towards a rich seam to be explored!

● **Where do they hang out?**
Which social media platforms do they frequent? What are their interests outside work? What industry groups are they in?

Chapter 8

Lifting the lid on sales flow management

O k, so you've nailed everything so far and your sales plan is working amazingly.

You have a growing list of contacts and regular enquiries for your products and/or services.

So how do you keep those enquiries coming in and more importantly, how do you turn them into sales?

Well this is called 'sales flow management' – we now need to explore this valuable concept and all it encompasses.

Introducing the Sales Funnel?

T he Sales Funnel represents the way your leads turn into prospects and then, from there, the prospects buy your product and turn into customers. This is all a natural progression of the sales process.

The funnel is widest at the top and becomes narrower as you get to the bottom. This is because not all leads become prospects, and not all prospects turn into customers. The funnel reflects the reality of the sales process and shows how you have to have more going in at the top to get anything coming out at the bottom. Simple really.

So – when we talk about Sales Funnels it's another way of describing the sales process.

And sales flow management is all about how you keep the prospects moving through the funnel until they buy your products and turn into customers!

Funnels and prospects

U sing a sales flow management system allows you to quickly identify at what stage your prospect is in the buying process. This will help you stop making the following, common mistakes:

1. You could try to close the sale too early – your prospect isn't ready to buy just yet and you may have put them off by being 'pushy.'

2. You could be talking to the wrong person – they don't have the say with the budget. Remember, you are only looking for prospects who have the gold you seek.

3. You could be pulling out too early – you give up calling because you haven't established what they need and when they need it.

4. You will experience a lot of wasted effort, and that means your time is lost money.

The need to set SMART targets

Anyone can pluck a figure out of the air and set a target. But there's far more to it than that. You need to know you can actually reach the target. You also need to know you've set the right target.

Your business needs to make money to grow so you need to ensure your sales targets underpin this.

Targets need to be **S.M.A.R.T.** This acronym breaks down as follows:

S: Targets have to be specific to make them useful in your business. To make it specific it has to say exactly what you want to achieve. Numbers and dates? How and by what method? What are you aiming for? Turnover? Units? Gross profit? – it's all about the detail.

M: There is a reason to make things measurable – and that is to be able to see if progress is being made – or not! A target that says 'I will be in profit by the end of next year' isn't measurable. Putting a number or a date against your target means that you can check if you are meeting your targets. Putting dates and numbers along the journey of the target also helps to check if you are making the progress you expect. If things are not on track you have the opportunity to make changes!

A: Can you actually reach your target? What will it take to make it happen? What resources will you need and is there the demand?
This is a 'sense check' moment that is necessary to make sure you are not setting yourself up to fail.

R: Is your target a relevant one – what this means is 'does it fit with your business goals and objectives?'
For example – If you have a business goal to extend your sales reach into Europe, then it is relevant to factor in movements in the Euro.

T: What is the timeline for the target? How long will it take and are there shorter time targets required to keep on track? Set times to check progress. Is this the right time? Should you delay? When will be the right time? Also, make sure everyone knows what needs to be done by when.

Take one of your targets and put it through the **SMART** process.

How specific is this target?	
Can you measure it?	
Is the target truly attainable?	
How relevant is this target to your business plans	
Have you laid out a timeline? When will this be completed?	

Setting **SMART** targets that work!

Define your targets, there is always more than one.

Whatever your business, selling things or services, you need to know what you want to achieve in both numbers and money.

How many do you need to sell to break even and how many to make a profit? How many to reach your targets?

The need for continued personal development

R emember at the beginning of this book we talked about growing your business and how it was like tending a garden? Well you can have the world's best horticultural tools, the very best seeds and soil people would kill for. But if you ain't got the skills and the knowledge your garden will still be a disaster.

It's the same in business – if you aren't prepared to continually arm yourself with the most up-to-date knowledge, you won't have a business.

Learn – Grow - Innovate

I t's true to say that we usually start our own business selling something that we are either already good at or have a passion for.

This means that we are quite often experts in our own field. We set up our business, we're buzzing with passion and we hit the ground running.

We're comfortable that we know our products or services better than the people we are selling to and our ego grows quickly. But this can be very dangerous – it can easily make you feel that personal development is not necessary.

But it's very easy to lay on your laurels and get left behind. It can happen so quickly. Just think how many industries have been left behind in the digital age. And just how many more will be left behind in the future.

To develop your business you must innovate and keep ahead of the game.

In the digital age, if you're not learning new techniques and technologies you will become obsolete.

Smaller businesses are at an advantage. The cost of training yourself and innovating the way you do things is minimal compared to larger competition.

You are the most vital resource in your business – you have to invest in yourself.

Invest time in reading and researching. There are trade magazines, self help books, online articles and blogs, YouTube, TED Talks. It's all at your fingertips in the online world.

Driving accountability – nothing happens without ACTION!

It doesn't matter if you are a one person business or have a whole team of employees working for you, it is important to have a structure that allocates responsibility for the tasks in hand.

This is what accountability is all about.

Imagine planning an event that needs a venue, catering, a cake, seating... you get the picture. Now imagine that you have 10 people to help you but you haven't had a detailed chat about who does what and by when – it's a recipe for disaster.

When things are not clearly explained and communicated, then you are likely to soon hear someone shouting 'It's not my fault' as things go wrong.

When things are not communicated clearly a project will simply fall apart and your goals/targets/objectives will be missed.

The key is to be specific.

And – if you are at all nervous about being that specific (because you maybe think it paints you as bossy?) then think about this:

When you are given a task to do by someone else, which is most comfortable?

1. You know a few details but it has been left to you to decide what needs to be done and when.

2. You have a clear schedule and understanding of what needs to be done by when and how.

The American Society of Training and Development did a study on accountability and found the probability of goal completion was higher or lower dependent on the following:

Probability of completion

when you have the idea or goal 10%

once you consciously decide you will do it = 25% probability of completion 25%

if you decide when you will do it = 40% probability of completion. 40%

when you plan how to do it = 50% probability of completion. 50%

once you commit to someone that you will do it = 65% probability of completion. 65%

when you have a specific accountability with a person you have committed to = 95% probability of completion. 95%

"The aim of life is self-development. To realise one's nature perfectly - that is what each of us is here for." – Oscar Wilde

It is very easy to list reasons why you can't or don't have the time or capacity to work on self-development. Here are a few you might have uttered yourself:
- "I don't know where to go to get help."
- "If I ask, I don't think they will let me."

- "I'm just too busy with work to write down my personal goals."
- "I don't have the confidence in myself."

These are simply excuses so don't use them.

Top tip #1: Be clear on what you want to improve.

The clearer and more precise you are to yourself about what it is you want to improve the easier it will be to set a goal. Sometimes, you may need to set a goal first to understand what it is you want to change or improve at. For example, rather than saying you want to know more about sales you could be more specific by saying you want to work on closing sales.

Top tip #2: Try to connect with other like-minded individuals.

Finding others who are working on the same self-development goals is a good way to hold yourself accountable e.g. agreeing to attend a course with them. Sharing common ground with others is also a good for staying motivated whilst also learning something you might not have found out on your own.

Top tip #3: Read, read and read some more.

Improvement comes from knowledge and understanding - knowledge and understanding comes from books, videos, podcasts and more. If sitting down with a book isn't the right way for you to learn about something, then watch videos or listen to podcasts instead. Basically, take advantage of all the free media out there to find out who to have as a virtual mentor. Then set some time each day or at least 5 days a week (even just 10 minutes) to learn more about your specific topic.

Top tip #4: Be resilient in creating good habits.

Deciding to make a change, setting self-development goals and telling someone else about them are all very good first steps towards enriching your knowledge and skillset. But ensure you think about the highs and lows. You are likely to hit speed bumps along the way. What will you do to overcome these and stay true to your intentions? Will you use a reward/sanction system, or will you find a role model to look to for inspiration when you hit a grey patch?

Top tip #5: Measure your progress against your self-development

goals.

An athlete runs a race with the finish line as the goal but in the longer-term they use the race times to compare against previous races to measure their progress. So it is true with your self-development whether that is personal or professional. Being able to measure where they are at allows the athlete the foresight to know when to change factors under their control, e.g. coach, diet, running gear, training regime, etc. If you have a self-development goal of closing sales, you could measure the number of sales closed as a percentage over a period of time such as 3 months.

Chapter 9

Re-programme your sales mindset for success

All really successful businesses continually evolve. They never stand still. They are always on the lookout for new ways to engage with customers and, as a result, sell more products and services.

Your sales mindset must never stop being on the look out for opportunities to keep your business ahead of the game.

And whilst you're doing this you must ensure you have the cashflow to keep your business moving forward. You will only do this if you're continually driving sales.

It's now time to delve into a method of managing the sales process to its optimum effect.

How to manage your sales using SPANCOP

This is a process I developed at Shell. It has become the cornerstone of my teachings. It's a method that lets you see exactly where each and every customer is in the sales process at any one time.

It stops you making stupid mistakes like discussing price before the customer is even comfortable with the solution to their problem you're offering.

Each of your customers will be sitting at one of seven steps mapped out by **SPANCOP**. So when you plot where your customers are you can see where you need to make effort in your business.

For example – if you have a lot of customers at order and payment stage, but not many at the suspect and prospect stage, then you will want to up your marketing and networking. **SPANCOP** ensures your sales pipeline runs like a well-oiled machine.

SPANCOP – your new best friend

There are huge benefits to having a more defined view of where your prospects are in the buying process - these are:

Focus: It helps you prioritise and track your target customers. You know where to spend your time. For example - got a prospect who has yet to be approached and analysed? You know it's time to make a call or book a meeting to move them on to the next stage.

Visibility: It will help you structure your sales flow pipeline growth more visibly. When you can see where your prospects are in the process you know where to direct your efforts. For example – lots of prospects stuck in one place? Not enough suspects and prospects to feed the funnel? You know what to do.

Discipline: Having a process makes you more disciplined and professional. You have a purpose in your sales process? You are managing your sales with discipline, making sure that everything has the best chance to develop and turn into a sale.

Opportunities: Knowing what is happening in your funnel means that you can manage both present and future opportunities. For example – when you can see that you have many prospects on the same buying timeline you can make sure you plan what you may need to do to promote customer retention once they have bought. It also means that you can spot marketing opportunities when they are needed.

Resources: Got a lot of customers all going through the funnel at the same time and at the same pace? You will only know this by using the SPANCOP method. This will allow you to have the right resource ready at the right time.

Relationships: Keeping in touch with your customers is a key activity. Knowing where your customer is in the process means you can tailor your conversation to where they are, avoiding the pitfalls of appearing too pushy or pulling out too early.

So let's dig down a bit further and investigate each of the seven stages of **SPANCOP**.

Suspect: A suspect is best characterised as someone who says they are interested in what you sell.

You may have met them at a networking event or they have liked your Facebook page

You don't know enough about this person's position to know if they're ready to buy at this point. But it's fair to say they're a warm lead.

You have to find out more about this person before considering them a prospect and moving to the next stage of the process.

It's fine to have conversations with a suspect, but it has to be with the intention of finding out if they are a prospect!

Prospect: Prospects are the buyers you are looking for – you will remember how to find and develop your prospects from the growth management chapter earlier.

Prospects have a budget.

Prospects have a problem that you have the solution for.

Prospects have the authority to buy.

Prospects may not be buying right now but they will be at some point in time so you need to know when they will be ready.

Prospects are worth your time and effort – they feed your sales funnel.

Approach and analyse: You have found your prospect and you know they have a problem in their business that your product or service can solve. Take some time to analyse and ask questions about the problem to make sure that your solution is a good fit. It's then time to approach them with your solution.

When approaching a prospect, focus on discussing their problems and offering possible solutions. This is not the appropriate time to discuss price, as you haven't yet established the value of the solution to them. Establish that your product or service is a good fit for their problem – help them to make that connection with features and benefits.

Negotiate: Once you have established you are a good fit for your prospect's problem you can now negotiate the price. The negotiation phase is where you can talk money. The prospect is now warmed up to the idea that they need what you have, so they are less likely to haggle on the price - provided you have set it appropriately for their budget of course.

You will know the value of your solution to their problem – if it makes (or saves) them money then the cost is a worthwhile investment for them.

None of this should be a surprise to you at this point in the process – you will have gained a good feel for their budget and the potential gain for them while you were working out if they were the right prospect for you.

Close: Closing the sale is where you gain the prospect's commitment to buy, so although money has not changed hands, it is at this point they are ready to confirm they will buy from you.

This is the time in the process to have patience – wait for the right time. Buying can be an anxious time for your prospect and they may need time to make sure they are making the right decision, especially if your sales strategy is low volume/high value.

Be careful not to seem too eager to close, it's just as you are about to close where buyers can have their last moment of doubt about whether to buy or not.

Be ready to answer more questions and listen to your prospect, they will buy in their own time – some quickly and some much more slowly.

Order: When your prospect is in the order phase then you are pretty much home and dry. It's at this point that you should already be thinking whether they will want to buy from you in the future. There's nothing better than repeat business! It's at this point where you can talk about future needs and orders. Regular order required? Yes please!

Payment: The last part of the **SPANCOP** process is the exchange of money - by whatever payment terms you have negotiated.

So congratulations - Your prospect has now become a customer!
You now need to answer some questions as you assess the process.
These are:
Are they now a repeat customer?
Are they still an ideal prospect?
What else may they need?
Have you planned in when you will talk to them again?

How to use **SPANCOP**

Inputting your customers into the **SPANCOP** process is pretty straightforward. Here are the basics.

1. Gather together all of the information you have on each of your suspects/prospects/customers. You will already have an idea of which category they fall into so start to plot some numbers. How many are suspects/prospects/customers?
2. Which suspects are likely to become prospects? Do you need to know more about them? Can you discard any now?
3. Where are your prospects in the buying process? Do you need to know more about them before you can place them?
4. Create a way of recording this information which will allow you to target your efforts, moving your prospects along the buying process.
   CRM software can be useful. Or you might opt for having a visible chart in your office or just building a useful spreadsheet.

Whatever way you choose, the way to use this process is for it to become a living, everyday activity for you to engage in.

SPANCOP Step	Which prospects are here	Next steps for each prospect
Suspect		
Prospect		
Approach and Analyse		
Negotiate		
Close		
Order		
Payment		

The **WOPPA** method of sales call/meeting planning

It's an old adage but a true one: failing to prepare is preparing to fail.

Planning your sales calls, meetings and other customer interactions is an absolute must if you are to make the most of each and every opportunity.

WOPPA is a simple acronym that helps you focus on the important elements of customer interactions like calls and meetings and keeps you on track to achieve your desired outcome.

It is a list of questions that prepares you for each call, meeting or interaction with a customer. Here's how it breaks down:

W: Why are you making this call or having this meeting? What is the purpose? If you don't know why then the whole interaction could just end up being a nice social call and nothing else.

O: What's the objective of the call? Be specific about what you expect the result of the customer interaction to be. Do you want to get an appointment or are you looking for an order? Is this a follow-up call or a post sales call? This will be governed by where your prospect is in the **SPANCOP** sales process.

P: Premise. This is where you bring in the things that you know about the prospect. How did your interaction end last time that is relevant to this interaction? For example – if your prospect was awaiting budget signoff the last time you spoke then this time you'll be calling to see the latter has been achieved.

P: Plan. Okay – it's a plan within a plan but this is all about your personal preparation. Here you are planning what you will do during the call or meeting. How do you tailor your approach to the prospect? What actions will you take? For example, will you need to make lots of notes? If so you have to remember to take a notebook and pen. Or do you need to research the prospect and their business to be prepared with some knowledge?

A: Anticipate. It's very likely that your prospect will have a lot of questions for you so this is a good time to spend anticipating what they may ask you. Again, this may depend on where they are in the sales process so make sure you have all bases covered.

So what are the additional benefits of using **WOPPA**?
• It builds confidence and gives greater clarity on what to achieve during a call or meeting.
• It allows you to be clear on the agenda you want to discuss.
• It maximises the time you spend with the prospect.

- It enables you to better measure success and anticipate the unexpected
- It drives a more consistent customer approach
- It provides structure to allow you to prepare for and achieve goals in a meeting or on a call

Why Why am I making this call or having this meeting?		
Objective What is my objective? What do I want the meeting to achieve?		
Plan What do I plan to do on the call?		
Premise What do I know about the prospect that can help me build a rapport.		
Anticipate What questions may they ask? How can I relieve any buyers anxiety?		

- It allows you to demonstrate professionalism and create confidence and trust in a customer's mind.
- It enables a customer interaction to run more smoothly.
- Sending the agenda in advance helps the prospect to prepare.

Take some time and plan out a sales call for your business. Role play it. Get comfortable with it. Get used to doing it. It make you more comfortable when you're doing the real thing.

Recording your sales calls and meeting outcomes

Unless you have the memory of an elephant then recording the outcomes and reviewing each customer interaction is a must.

You should create a file on each and every prospect. You need to remember everything about them.

Every call and interaction is an addition to that file. This information will guide your next steps and help you process what you learned.

If you don't capture this information quickly you will forget it. Recording details of an interaction within 12 hours is the optimum time. Any later than this and you'll forget things and miss important elements that will assist the prospect's smooth movement through the sales pipeline.

Here's an example of what can happen when you don't record and review:
"I tried to call Mr Smith from Widgets.com again this morning but his secretary told me he was on holiday – totally forgot that he was planning to go to France. I also wasn't sure what we talked about last time so I felt a bit awkward about making the call and put it off a couple of days – did he say he needed to get the budget?"

And here's an example of what happens when you do record and review:
"Called Mr Smith at Widgets.com and he was ready to talk about orders.
So glad that I had put in his file that he was going to be on holiday and would be getting the budget signed off while he was away in France. We agreed on one more meeting to firm up the details – see him in two weeks to talk numbers".

A brief synopsis of the conversation today	
Where is my prospect now in SPANCOP after that conversation?	
Have I been speaking to the right person? If not, who is the right person?	
Can I fulfil the prospects needs in the timescale?	
Was this the best time to contact them? if not, when is better?	
When will I speak to them next?	
Did I get an Order? If not, when is it likely?	
Do I have any concerns about credit terms?	

Creating your prospect files

There are a number of ways to create prospect files.
You may like the traditional pen and paper approach or something more technical and online. Using CRM software is a great option and very efficient.

There is no right or wrong format – just as long as it gets done. Nothing happens without action!

Whichever way you do it – here are the basic areas that you must capture as quickly as possible after the call or meeting:

• Where is my prospect now in my **SPANCOP** sales process? Can I move them to the next level? What are the next steps for this prospect?

• Have I been speaking to the right person? If not, who is the right person? How will I know they are the right person?

• Can I fulfil the prospect's needs in the timescale we have talked about? Was this the best time to talk to them and when should I speak to them next?

• Did I get an order? When am I likely to get an order? Do I have the capacity to take an order?

• Do I have any concerns about credit for this prospect? Are they a good credit risk? What will my terms be?

Exercise

Capture the outcomes of your next call or meeting. Get used to doing it. Make it a habit.

Chapter 10

Customer retention

Did you know it's seven times more expensive to find a new client than to keep an existing one? Think about that before you let a good client drift off into the ether. It takes a lot of work to get them!

If you think about how much time and effort it takes to move someone from suspect to payment in your pipeline, you can begin to understand why.

Combatting CHURN

The **CHURN** rate for a business is the number of clients you lose in a given period of time. Let's assume that you work with 12-month contracts with your clients. The **ANNUAL CHURN** rate for your business will be the percentage of your clients that leave after the 12-month contract expires.

If you have 100 clients on 12-month contracts, and 5 of them don't renew, your **CHURN** rate is 5%.

Knowing (or even just having a rough idea of) your **CHURN** rate is useful to set yourself a target of new clients to at least maintain the income you have from your existing clients.

Cross-sell, up-sell, re-sell and more – five ways to sell again!

You have already invested a lot of effort turning a prospect into a customer so it makes sense to maximise that opportunity to sell to them again. There are five main ways to do this.

Cross-sell

Do you have a range of products in your 'ecosystem'? It is very likely that your customer has a need for at least one other of the products in your range – they just don't know it yet!

It is useful to introduce your other products early on in the buying process to further understand your customer's buying needs. For example, if you sell health products you should create opportunities to talk about things that may complement the product they already have a need for.

Up-sell

This method works brilliantly if you have developed a product eco-system and have a range of products/services at differing costs.

For example - you might have a premium product that offers greater value but at greater cost. Where a first-time buyer might not trust you enough to make such a significant investment, an existing client may well do. Further down the line you should be able to tempt the first-time buyer to invest further and move to a premium product.

Re-sell

No customer should be allowed to leave you without being asked about future buying opportunities. Asking for repeat business is a basic so make sure that this is done during the COP stage of SPANCOP. Keeping in touch post sale is a vital way of maintaining the relationship and making sure that the customer is aware of any new products or offers you may have, so make sure this is factored into your post call reviews.

Recommendation

Satisfied and loyal customers provide the best advertising you will ever get as they recommend you to friends and family. Make sure you look after them! Your customer feedback and post sale contact will help you keep your existing customer base working for you.

Innovations

Your customers are a great source of ideas for new products and product improvements. You will already be getting customer feedback so you can use it to focus on what else customers may want that you don't already provide. Also, look at how you can create a variety of levels of product from basic to premium. For example - customer focus groups. There are lots of ideas out there to help make this happen.

How do I deal with complaints?		
How can I have regular contact with my customers?		
Is my Retention strategy feeding into my Marketing?		
How do I know if customers have recommended me?		
Have I special offers for loyal customers?		
Do I know what my customer CHURN rate is and what am I doing about it?		

This is a question I've been asked a thousand times! And the answer provides incredibly useful information so take note of it.

First things first - don't land at your desk at 9am on a Monday morning fired up to make sales calls. Your week will likely be in ruins by 9.01am and your motivation levels will have dropped onto the minus scale! It doesn't matter how prepared you are – it will be a disaster. Here's the likely conversation:

"Hello?"

"Oh, hi there, I was wondering if I'd be able to speak to Michelle?"

"This is Michelle, can I ask who's calling please?"

"Hi, Michelle, it's Steve, I just wondered if you have a couple of minutes at the moment so I can show you how I can help you with my new online service?"

"Sorry, Steve, now's not a good time, sorry I'm really busy."

"Is there a better time t-"

"Sorry, Steve I've got to go....Thanks David can you just put it on my desk?"
Call Ended
00:00:57.

So what went wrong? Well everything really.

You only thought about yourself. You were ready to make the call but Michelle had just gotten in after a weekend break away and she was in the middle of starting to catch up with everything. The staff in the office hadn't been able to get hold of her over the weekend – an urgent issue had come up - so as soon as she got in on Monday morning, she was inundated with work.

The last thing she had time for was a sales call. Have a think about your

average Monday morning. 'To do' lists are likely to be weighing heavily. You probably won't come up for air until the afternoon at the earliest! The last thing you want is someone bending your ear with a sales call.

The best days to cold call?
Thursday is statistically the best day.
Wednesday the second best.
Tuesday is the worst day for sales calls – and Monday morning should be avoided at all costs.
So that's it – you should be making your sales calls on a Thursday or Wednesday.

The best times to cold call?
The best times for a sales call is between 4pm and 5pm – people are beginning to wind down and their 'to do' lists for that day are largely done.
The next best times are between 8am and 10am – just before people really kick into their working day as they're more likely to be reading blogs and catching up with social media. The worst times to cold call are between 11am and 2:00pm. People are now in the hectic flow of the working day.
Sometimes it's the simple things that become the barriers to making sales!

Are you familiar with the term 'the gatekeeper'. If you've ever done any 'cold calling' I'm sure you are!
This the individual whose job it is to prevent people getting access to the decision-maker.
Typically, this is a personal assistant or a secretary, but in some companies, it is even the receptionist or switchboard operator.
So below are my tips on how best to circumnavigate them and give you a bit more insight into their role and why - even though you're trying to get beyond them - they are there for a reason and they have an important job to do.

Tip 1: the gatekeeper is not the enemy
Whoever is acting as the gatekeeper between you and the decision-maker (DM) is just doing their job. Part of that job is managing demands on the DM's

time. Seeing the gatekeeper as the enemy creates a barrier that it will be difficult to remove.

Tip 2: Sound senior

Management never gets treated the same as the workers. If someone believes that you are important, they will treat you differently. Using a relaxed and calm voice, speak slowly and articulately and don't divulge more than is necessary. During the opening seconds of your conversation, if the gatekeeper senses that you are their senior, they will not risk offending you by probing too deeply.

Tip 3: The gatekeeper is a wealth of knowledge

Remember that whilst the gatekeeper's role is to restrict interruptions to the DM's daily routine, they do know a great deal of important information about the DM and the business. Use this opportunity to check that the person that you want to speak to is the decision-maker. Check your facts with them. Ask simple, non-intrusive open questions to try to build up a picture of both the gatekeeper and the decision-maker.

Tip 4: Don't sell

The gatekeeper has several distinct 'powers'. One of them is the power to connect you with the right person. However, they do not hold any decision-making powers. When the gatekeeper asks "Can I tell him/her what it's regarding?"

– do not try to pitch your product or service to the gatekeeper. Firstly, it will waste your time. Second, it will irritate them because they will just be waiting for an opportunity to tell you that they cannot help you. No matter how desperate to connect with the DM you are, do not sell to the gatekeeper.

Tip 5: Engage don't evade
Don't be awkward, don't try to sneak past them, the chances are you'll get cut off at the knees. Actively engage with the gatekeeper. Don't get too personal, don't pry, but you can gently probe. If you can't get through to the DM, engage the gatekeeper so that they have a positive and friendly attitude towards you when you call again. You're unlikely to become best friends, but building a relationship and a rapport with them will help them want to help you.

Tip 6: Easy does it
If you are nervous, stressed or tense, you will transfer those feelings to your voice, your behaviour and choice of words. All of these will make an impact on how the gatekeeper perceives you and I how they receive your request for access or information. Take some deep slow quiet breaths in through the nose and out through the mouth to put yourself at ease. When the gatekeeper answers, smile and confidently greet them with energy and ease.

Tip 7: Don't script, but have a plan
Unless you are a particularly good actor, don't use a script. They are likely to hear the scripted tone in your voice. Instead, plan how you will approach them; what approaches you might take depending upon the range of responses that they might make. Plan your responses to key objections but leave yourself room by improvising the dialogue.

Tip 8: Is the DM expecting your call?
In order to bypass the gatekeeper, use the DM's first name only. Ask "Can I speak to Sarah please?", it sounds like a personal call. Remember your goal is not to inform the gatekeeper; your goal is to bypass them to get to the DM. Next, they might ask "Is she expecting your call?". Simply and easily reply "Yes, I sent her some information through from our head office, we need to discuss it before close of business today."

Chapter 11

21st century TV sales stereotypes –

which side turns you on?

It's interesting how business and entrepreneurship has come into the mainstream in recent years via two very high profile TV shows – Dragon's Den and the Apprentice.

One has single-handedly perpetuated the negative stereotype of sales and the other – well I'm glad to say it regularly backs up a lot in this book.

Can you hazard a guess which one? You don't have to be Einstein to decide if you've caught the shows.

The Apprentice reality TV show takes its contestants to hell and back as they sell their souls to get a sale in a series of regularly demeaning tasks.

Many have called it the business world's answer to 'Big Brother' as they all share a house like in the mainstream reality TV show.

The Apprentice contestants will seemingly stoop to any level to get a sale in a bid to win the show's prize – a chance to work for the show's UK presenter Alan Sugar.

Many would argue the programme has changed the world. It started in the USA before it hit UK shores with none other than Donald Trump as host.

His profile skyrocketed due to the success of the show and many say it provided the platform for his eventual success in the US elections.

Considering the opinions of many regarding the way he conducts his presidency (and his life) it's unlikely his image connected with a programme influencing sales stereotypes in the 21st century will ever be a positive one with everyone.

The UK version of the show fronted by Sir Alan Sugar hardly enhances the image of the salesperson either.

Do you remember very early on in this book that a lightbulb moment for me was the realisation that a sale had to provide equal value for both sides?

Well think back to the Apprentice as the teams are pitted against each other as they race to make the most sales.

Do you think they display the image of someone striving for a win: win situation? Nope, all they want to do is sell the most and win the programme. The buyer's thoughts appear largely inconsequential much of the time.

Dragon's Den is different entirely. They examine products and concepts and decide if they are a good fit with the market.

They want to know that entrepreneurs have researched their businesses to the enth degree – they want success for the products.

They're looking for ideas and businesses with robust sales and marketing plans. They're on the look out for sustainable and growing businesses as the Dragons – a bunch of mega-rich entrepreneurs themselves – are weighing up whether they will invest in them or not.

At one time it was thought the popularity of both programmes would kick off a whole wave of new, would-be entrepreneurs coming into the market place for the first time.

But many would argue the very opposite has happened.

The media's appetite to entertain has totally subverted the appeal of entrepreneurship. In fact a study by Salford University Business School concluded both shows promoted 'an unhealthy level of ruthlessness and arrogance' and fostered misconceptions about the traits required for business success.

So it's fair to say things have moved on regarding the image of sales in some respects – but there's still a long way to go.

I'm actually a member of the Association of Professional Sales and I'm a keen supporter of the lobby working towards a charter mark for the industry by 2020.

I want some formal recognition for my industry! I hope the industry will get your support once you're comfortable with selling.

truly hope you've found this book useful and insightful. I'm a big believer in simplicity and providing practical, easy to follow information.

I'm honoured to say my teachings have helped hundreds of businesses and

Chapter 12

Conclusions and where next?

the number is growing all the time.

Everything is tried and tested – by me! The methods in this book helped Shell grow its market share in the mining sector of South Africa from 43% to 82% in just 2.5 years.

And remember – that multi-million dollar industry with thousands of employees wasn't something that could be changed fast.

SMEs are at an advantage – they're lean and can implement changes quickly.

But one thing rings true time and time again.

To succeed you must take action. You must change your sales mindset so my teachings become part of your everyday working life.

Only then will you have truly embraced sales and the fortunes of your business will start to transform.

Sales – like any other area of business – is one that never stands still. Technology has been a game changer for it.

I meet scores of business that haven't adapted to the digital age – their lack of progress can easily see them put out of business.

I see many traditional manufacturing companies relying on sales and marketing strategies of 30 years ago.

It is so easy to be left behind. Don't let that become you. You need to own the business space you're in and you only do that by staying ahead of the competition.

And take solace in the fact that I'm still on that development journey with you! I know the importance of staying ahead of the competition and keeping ahead of changes within the industry.

I learn from my mistakes and continually push forward with new ideas. Some will work – some won't.

Further developments are my own CRM system which I'm hoping you'll have access to in the future.

If you've tried any of the existing ones you'll probably find – even though they have infinite numbers of uses – they're way too complex for the average SME owner.

So watch this space! I've also developed my very own board game which again is a really exciting concept to further help people learn and feel comfortable with the sales process.

If you've just finished this book I know you've an exciting journey ahead as you start to instil my teachings into your life and business.

But I know change doesn't always happen overnight and sometimes you need like-minded people to bounce ideas off and share your frustrations as you move forward.

So why not join my free Sales Mindset Group on Faceboook? You'll find hundreds of like-minded people with exactly the same issues as you!

If you want a tailor made programme to truly take things to the next level why not become a student of my online Accelerator Programme?

You'll find details at www.thesalesmindsetcoach.com

And ensure you sign up to my blog for regular tips and updates.

If you want to speak to me personally why not drop me a line at steve@thesalesmindsetcoach.com – I do my best to answer every email myself.

You can also catch me on Twitter - @MindsetForSales

Don't forget you can download all the Funnel Vision – Selling Made Easy assets here: https://thesalesmindsetcoach.com/funnel-vision-assets/

Last word:

Sometimes things happen for a reason and you'll definitely find that on your sales journey. Your mindset won't change overnight but it will change as you follow my teachings – you business world will transform.

I thought I was the king of sales when I was at Calor and it's only looking back that I realise I'd hardly started! I thought I was more than worthy of sales manager and I got my ego well and truly cut down to size when I didn't get the position.

But wow – if it hadn't been for that rejection I would have never had landed the job at Shell and I definitely wouldn't be writing this book now. So if at first you don't succeed – read my book again and again until you do. And if that doesn't work – drop me an email!

Glossary

Suspect: Someone you suspect might be a potential prospect.

Prospect: Someone you know is one hundred per cent in the market for what you're selling.

Cold call: Making contact with someone that has no prior knowledge of your product or service.

Warm call: Making contact with someone that has prior knowledge of your product or service.

Lead: A potential prospect.

PEAR planning: A method of building your sales plan.

SPANCOP: My sales planning process.

WOPPA: A method of keeping track of your sales process.

CHURN rate: How regularly you lose clients and business.

You can find the Funnel Vision – Selling Made Easy assets here:
https://thesalesmindsetcoach.com/funnel-vision-assets/

Lightning Source UK Ltd.
Milton Keynes UK
UKHW021217021119
352725UK00006B/56/P